What people are saying about this handbook:

"I have experienced Dr. Shaw's warm and challenging presence in her sexuality workshop and used her workbook with patients and in my workshops for gay men: *Through Shame and Idealization to Love.* I am repeatedly impressed by, and very grateful for, the depth and integrity of her approach to enriching this vital area of men's lives. She brings together permission for playfulness, support for significant vulnerability, and personal growth. She grounds these challenges in rich understanding of the separation and individuation required for deepening relational intimacy. Her honesty, humanity, insight, and humor are a gift to us all."

— David M. Hawkins, M.D.
Director, Group Psychotherapy Training Program
Duke University Medical Center, Chapel Hill, NC
President, American Group Psychotherapy Association
Past President, American Academy of Psychotherapists

"This user friendly, innovative handbook for male couples can be highly effective in reviving eroticism and intimacy together. It is sex affirmative and poised for couples at the turn of the century."

— Andrew Mattison, M.S.W., Ph.D.
Co-author, *The Male Couple: How Relationships Develop*
Departments of Psychiatry and Family Medicine
University of California, San Diego

"To my knowledge, this is the first practical workbook for gay couples. The manual's emphasis and value is in viewing sex not simply as behavior designed to achieve intense orgasms, but as an important element of intimate communication between two men. The author, a gifted sex therapist, makes an important contribution to the enhancement and viability of gay marriages."

— Stuart Strenger, Ph.D.
Clinical Psychologist

Journey
Toward Intimacy
A Handbook for Gay Couples

Jeanne Shaw, Ph.D.

Revised Edition

Couples Enrichment Institute
P. O. Box 420114
Atlanta, Georgia 30342-0114

Journey Toward Intimacy

A Handbook for Gay Couples

Jeanne Shaw, Ph.D.

Published by:

The Couples Enrichment Institute
P.O. Box 420114
Atlanta, Georgia 30342-0114 USA

Printed in the United States of America

ISBN 1-891257-06-4

Library of Congress Catalogue Card Number 98-92434

Forward

During the late 1960s and throughout 1970, gay men experienced a long-awaited metamorphosis in sexuality that was unprecedented historically. The explosion of sexual freedom and expression occurred as the result of a few courageous men who found thousands and then millions of gay men ripe for revolution and transformation. We were beginning to escape a lifetime of severe and painful repression and sexual suppression. Our closet doors opened, some with a bang and some ever so gingerly. For many, open and free sexual expression became synonymous with claiming a heretofore deadened part of ourselves.

The battle for equal rights, acceptance, and respect was now out in the open. Evidence of this ongoing campaign is readily seen in our daily lives. Our gains are enormous and celebrated with pride. Yet, the struggles before us can, at times, seem overwhelming and insurmountable. During the 1980s, we suddenly found ourselves in shock from the newly identified HIV. The reward of our brand new freedom was quickly threatened by this deadly disease. How tragic were the thousands of losses. And still further tragic that sexual expression became so intimately tied to fear for our lives.

It is from within this complex atmosphere that gay men are struggling to explore and understand their sexual selves. How do we find the closeness, intimacy, and erotic connection that is ultimately the most satisfying? Do we find it by looking to different partners? Do we find it by looking to different atmospheres? Do we find it by being exclusive? Do we find it by trying different sexual activities? Do we find it by digging more deeply into our vulnerability?

In my personal experience as a gay man, in talking with my gay friends, and in working deeply with gay men in individual, couples, and group therapy, I have participated in and/or witnessed this searching in many different directions. Each gay man, whether in partnership or alone, is struggling to find connection. Some are successful in their pursuits while others are barely holding on. My awareness of and involvement in this ongoing process highly motivates me to seek structures and mechanisms that will help us all get more of what we need and want.

Hence, I appreciate the invitation from Dr. Jeanne Shaw to review, react to, and edit this manual for gay couples. I am excited about the wisdom she shares from her years of experience in working with couples. She offers us a format that most certainly offers an incredibly useful vehicle to deepen our relationships. I strongly believe that working through this manual will provide many answers and directions that gay men so hopefully desire.

David E. Loftis, Ph.D.
Clinical Psychologist
1997

Contents

Warning — Disclaimer

This book is meant to provide information to male couples on the subject matter covered. It is sold with the understanding that the publisher and author are not engaged in rendering professional services through this handbook. Although it may be used in conjunction with therapy, it does not take the place of therapy. If counseling is required, please use a *licensed* mental health professional.

It is not within the scope of this handbook to provide complete information on the topic. You are urged to read available material about gay relationships and tailor the information to your own needs. For more material, please see the section on Suggested Readings, page 103.

Every effort has been made to make this handbook concise and accurate. However, standards of couples' sexual behavior change with social change, so concepts basic to this handbook may change over time.

The purpose of this handbook is to educate and inspire you toward fulfilling your sexual potential. The author and Couples Enrichment Institute have neither liability nor responsibility to any person or couple with respect to any loss or damage caused or alleged to have been caused, directly or indirectly, by your choice to use the information contained herein.

If you do not wish to be bound by the above, you may return this book unused to the publisher for a full refund.

Welcome to the Handbook!

Journey Toward Intimacy is a handbook for gay couples who want a lasting, erotic, intimate sexual relationship, as well as for couples who are bored or unfulfilled. It introduces partners to new perspectives about being sexually intimate with each other whether the relationship is sexually exclusive or includes other people.

Most male couples early in a relationship experience hot sex; they play, enjoy each other, and occasionally use sex toys, fantasy, and erotica to enhance the intensity of their genital experience. Intense orgasms are usually part of courtship. However, creating enduring sexual satisfaction and an increasingly erotic relationship requires emotional risk-taking and personal integrity beyond seeking stronger, more intense genital stimulation.

The following exercises may assist you in discovering something about yourself as well as your partner. The exercises were originally designed for weekend workshops where partners explore and restore sexual energy and gain new perspectives about developing as a couple. You can arrange to do these exercises over time, or do them in a concentrated way in your own self-regulated sexual retreat.

The active pursuit of sexual contact in and out of relationship is natural to men. Gay men in relationships can experience both freedom and anxiety with inclusive sex, that is, including others in your sex life. This freedom, however, comes not only with a sense of entitlement, but with responsibility to yourself and your partner. Partners must decide how, and under what circumstances, they will include or exclude others sexually. Couples must also consider what happens when one partner changes his mind.

Expressing yourself sexually in a long-term relationship is developmental work, an adventure, and an encounter with your sexual potential. The simple part is understanding your and your partner's sexual energy, both for connecting and for sexual expression. The hard part is discovering whether genital familiarity enhances or dilutes your development, and whether it focuses you on genital sensations to the inclusion or exclusion of intimate feelings.

These pages might guide you into new conceptual territory about sex. Couples report that the exercises are rewarding, eye-opening, and anxiety-producing. The exercises are not sex manual techniques, but guideposts for erotic experience with a life partner. There is no wrong way to approach these exercises; however, following the guidelines in sequence can enrich your journey.

Guidelines:

1. Read the suggestions at the beginning of each exercise and do the exercise.

2. Make time with your partner to compare responses.

3. Don't explode, don't cave in, and don't leave. Just quiet yourself.

4. After each discussion, talk about how it was for you to consider the topic. *This is vital.*

Purposes

This handbook was written to help you:

1. Observe how beliefs and attitudes affect your sexual enthusiasm for yourself and your partner.

2. Learn how knowing yourself can lead you to sexual intimacy and lasting erotic energy.

3. Recognize the thoughts, feelings, and behaviors that enhance or block sexual energy and expression.

4. Contrast your anxiety-reducing behaviors (safe, familiar, and comfortable) and intimate behavior (risky, unfamiliar, and uncomfortable).

5. Emphasize erotic intimacy more than fantasy, sex toys, or sex games.

6. Learn how partner-validation builds good-will and how self-validation builds maturity and sexual energy.

7. Recognize the difference between closeness and intimacy.

8. Explore your capacity for maturity and erotic intimacy in relationship.

Bon Voyage!

Before reading further, compose your responses to the following ideas and share them with your partner:

My wish for *myself* in completing this handbook:

My wish for *you* in completing this handbook:

My desire for our *relationship*:

I am open to new perspectives for our relationship:

    ☐ yes   ☐ no

Other comments to my partner:

Sexual Attitudes

The next page is a survey of sexual attitudes. Attitudes, values, and beliefs can support or weaken sexual energy and desire. Sexual attitudes have meaning that affects your choices and directs your behavior. When you explore attitudes together, you create options for sexual enrichment. Talking together openly while being fully present allows you and your partner to know each other deeply. Being mature enough to know and accept each other accelerates sexual energy. Presence invites emotional intimacy and the sexual options intimacy allows, a wonderfully positive sequence.

Your attitudes are especially important when they cause conflict because conflict invites reflection. Conflict not only helps you know you are a separate person with different ideas and feelings from your partner, it pushes you to define yourself and revise your thinking at the same time. Defining, reflecting, and revising are tasks of maturity.

Play, playfulness, and laughter are effective ways to know each other. Playing lets you get close enough and erotic enough to experience intimate sex as qualitatively different from orgasmic relief. Intimacy is a choice, not between orgasm or connection, but to have orgasms *with* connection. The ability to feel related during sex is a task of maturity.

Self-awareness is the first step toward being a fulfilled sexual partner. Self-awareness helps you identify your attitudes, including those that help and those that hurt. When you are clear about your own attitudes, you create options for putting and getting more of what you want in your relationship.

Another mature task is letting your partner know how you experience yourself in relationship with him. Talking about something vulnerable and complex might go against your inclinations; however, you can learn to discuss difficult topics without over-reacting, caving in, or leaving, emotionally or physically.

Suggestions:

1. Fill out the *Sexual Attitude Survey*. Choose quickly and spontaneously. There are no wrong answers, only useful information.

2. Make enough time to compare responses. Each partner's response will have a unique meaning.

3. You can learn the most from the areas where you differ. Difference can trigger uneasiness, which, in turn, opens opportunities to deepen intimacy. Either partner can ask, "Am I OK with difference?" "How do I manage my uneasiness *with him* instead of without him?" Managing unease helps erotic development.

4. Notice where you agree. Agreement offers the comfort necessary for the survival of a relationship.

5. Don't explode, don't cave in, and don't leave. Just quiet yourself. Continue talking until you feel finished or agree to continue later. Honor your agreement.

6. Afterwards, talk about what it was like to discuss your sexual attitudes.

Sexual Attitude Survey

Indicate whether you Agree or Disagree:

( )   1. Sex is perfect in every way, there is nothing I need to change (skip this question if you fell in love recently).

( )   2. By now, my partner should be sensitive enough to know what turns me on without my having to say anything.

( )   3. Sexual pleasure should be easy and spontaneous.

( )   4. I sometimes surprise myself with new ways to make love.

( )   5. I tell him what pleasures me sexually and what doesn't.

( )   6. At times in my life I have had sex when I really did not want to, just to please my partner.

( )   7. I often enhance my arousal by having a sexual fantasy while having sex with my partner.

( )   8. I wish I could ignore my partner's desire for sex, but he tries so hard to please me that I feel guilty saying no.

( )   9. I could behave more erotically if I thought he could handle it.

( ) 10. I can tell when my partner is turned on to a fantasy instead of to me.

( ) 11. Sex for me is often monotonous or for release.

( ) 12. I want to give my partner what he wants but neither he nor I know what that is.

( ) 13. Something is missing sexually that I cannot name.

( ) 14. I feel confident about my ability to arouse him.

( ) 15. I usually don't say how I feel when I think he will get upset or respond in a way that makes me anxious.

( ) 16. I want to explore being more uninhibited with him.

( ) 17. I understand the meaning and terms of sexual exclusivity in our relationship.

( ) 18. He should want sex or agree to it when I want it.

( ) 19. To enjoy sex, I first need to feel emotionally connected.

( ) 20. To feel emotionally connected, I first need to enjoy sex.

( ) 21. When conflict arises, I use it to clear the air.

( ) 22. I hate responding to this questionnaire.

( ) 23. A statement I wish had been included:

Common Misinformed Beliefs About Sex

The next exercise is a brief list of common erroneous beliefs about sex, any one of which can block sexual enjoyment. Almost everybody in our culture learns, without meaning to, that natural sexuality is shameful, and gay sexuality even more so. You can shift these attitudes by observing your own sexual beliefs and values, then convert them to suit who you are now. Questioning and correcting misinformation about sex increases your options to behave sexually. You can confront misinformation most effectively when you do it gently and respectfully in conversation with your partner. Knowing whether your beliefs are the result of shame and anxiety, and whether they create distance, helps you change them.

You may benefit from reading a good sex education book (your partner can tell you if you would benefit). SIECUS, AASECT (see Community Resources, page 105), gay bookstores, newsletters, Lambda, and the Suggested Reading section in the appendix of this book can help you locate accurate sex education references.

Sex education and erotica are not equivalent. Sex education teaches you about your body and how it operates, offers specific information for sexual skills and problems, and gives you permission to feel sexual with your partner. The purpose of sex education is to educate; the purpose of erotica is to arouse. Erotic sexual arousal is learned, revised, and relearned at increasingly higher levels. With increasingly erotic sex with the same partner over many years, you gain in ability to manage anxiety and emotional discomfort.

The next pages describe some of the more common, often stereotypical beliefs men have about their sexuality and its expression. Following that list are brief commentaries based on today's social beliefs and biological data.

Suggestions:

1. First, decide whether each belief is "true" or "false" according to your own beliefs.

2. Review and compare responses. Then, together, read the commentary that follows.

3. Major disagreements about ideas make for fertile discussions. Decide what holding different views means to each of you, how differences affect your thinking, sexual behavior, and sexual energy.

4. Don't explode, don't cave in, and don't leave. Just quiet yourself.

5. Afterwards, talk about how it was for you to discuss your misconceptions. Was it difficult, easy, stirring, boring, enjoyable, insightful, risky?

Common Misinformed Beliefs About Sex

☐ When he's hard he's sexually aroused by *me*.

☐ Unless he has an erection, he doesn't love me.

☐ If we love each other and communicate, good sex will follow naturally.

☐ Sexual problems mean something is wrong in the relationship.

☐ Casual sex is more exciting than intimate sex with my long term partner.

☐ In a good sexual relationship, I should have a fulfilling experience each time.

☐ After age 25, sex drive decreases and stops altogether by age 65.

☐ It is the top's role to initiate.

☐ If either partner is aroused, oral and anal sex must follow.

☐ When you lose sexual desire, the best remedy is to find more partners.

☐ People with partners should not masturbate.

☐ The best sex is spontaneous and unplanned.

☐ Both partners should have high sexual desire for sex to be enjoyable.

☐ Sexual give and take is always equal and reciprocal.

☐ The best orgasm with your lover is with your eyes closed, having a sexual fantasy.

☐ A large penis indicates a sexually skilled man.

☐ Anal sex is the only sex that really counts.

☐ If I cannot make him ejaculate, I must be an inadequate lover.

Commentary on Common Misinformed Beliefs About Sex

When he's hard he's sexually aroused by me. Not necessarily. He may be aroused by his fantasy. Erections happen for many reasons, including nonsexual ones such as anxiety. And yes, he may be turned on to you.

Unless he has an erection he doesn't love me. While an erection may mean he is sexually aroused, it is not an indication of love. He can love you without an erection. Your sense of loving and being loved should depend on your experience, not on an erection.

If we love each other and communicate, good sex will follow naturally. While communication is necessary, it is not sufficient for good sex. Some men focus on sex to *avoid* communication and intimacy. Some prefer feeling close before they engage in sex. Some feel intimate as a result of sex. Actually, you cannot NOT communicate, no matter how sex goes.

Sexual problems mean something is wrong in the relationship. Relationships without problems can get stale, and some couples have good sex even with problems. A sexual problem may be the result of a relationship problem, a medical condition, or an indication that partners are ripe for further development. Certain prescription and over-the-counter medicines contribute to sexual problems. This should be evaluated by a physician knowledgeable in sexual pharmacology and sexual medicine.

Casual sex is more exciting than intimate sex with my long-term partner. Although casual sex can be highly intimate in the moment, it is not enduring for many men. Casual sex eventually becomes boring, inducing more attention to penile stimulation than to experience with your partner.

In a good sexual relationship I should have a fulfilling experience each time. No, you should have an *experience* each time. You might not even have an orgasm each time, especially as you age. Everything in life has cycles, including sex, which can be awful, awesome, monotonous, good-enough, mind-blowing, regrettable, and unbelievably erotic.

After age 25, sex drive decreases and stops altogether by age 65. Not true. Your "jack-rabbit" ability wanes after the twenties and levels off until midlife, when you can become sexually skilled with your whole mind and body, not just your penis. Beyond 55 or so, time between orgasms may increase, the angle widens between your erect penis and stomach, and the number of orgasmic contractions decrease. However, sexual pleasure remains. A decreasing sex drive should be checked by a physician knowledgeable in sexual medicine, whatever your age.

It is the top's role to initiate. Both partners can decide who initiates, when, and under what circumstances. Or, it can be "understood" when it has been made explicit, previously, by both of you. When you rely on stereotypical or gay cultural beliefs about how to conduct sex, you limit your adventure, pleasure, and personal growth. Deciding how to decide is a vital issue.

If either partner is aroused, oral or anal sex must follow. Arousal is a state to be enjoyed, not performed. Arousal can be ignored, joined, or observed as partners express themselves sexually. An erection is not a demand. Disappointment is manageable.

When you lose sexual desire, the best remedy is to find another partner. This misguided solution preserves the myth that someone else is responsible for your sexuality. The best remedy is to sexualize and liberate yourself in the relationship you have. Losing desire for your partner is a signal to turn up the pilot light of being more yourself, with him.

People with partners do not masturbate. Of course they do. They just don't often discuss it if it seems private, shameful, or against the rules. Masturbation is not a substitute for partner sex, it is sex with yourself. Include your partner anytime you like. Mutual masturbation and observation is not only safer for HIV+ partners, it is one of the more intimate behaviors couples can do together.

The best sex is spontaneous and unplanned. Only people without jobs, financial obligations, or responsibilities for a home believe this. Even spontaneous sex is planned (e.g., brush your teeth, put on a cock ring). The best sex is planned with happy anticipation.

Both partners should have high desire for sex to be enjoyable. High desire is fine but not realistic. One partner should have enough desire to invite the other's participation. Desire can be as simple as being willing to participate (but not as a duty).

Sexual give and take is always equal and reciprocal. Giving and taking are individual decisions, not reciprocal duties. You may give sexually because you enjoy "doing" your partner, but giving may mean letting your partner "do" you. If you give only to get, your partner will soon feel used poorly.

The best orgasm with a lover is with eyes closed, having a fantasy. Fantasy-dependent sex is masturbation, not love-making. Fantasy can be a fun, occasional divergence, but it is disconnecting when it happens most of the time.

A large penis indicates a sexually skilled man. Size does not predict level of sexual energy, attraction, or skill.

Anal sex is the only sex that counts. This myth creates performance anxiety and sustains the misbelief that a man is only as good as his penis or his anus.

If I cannot make him ejaculate I'm not performing well. Your performance is not what his orgasm depends on. His connection with himself while he is with you is what makes him ejaculate, even though you are stimulating him physically. You are responsible only for your own pleasure and skill as a lover. He is, likewise, responsible. You can share his feelings and thoughts, not his genitals. Thinking about your performance means you are not fully present, sexually, but thinking, instead. Just enjoy him without feeling obligated to perform. He can make himself ejaculate later, if he so desires, and you can watch.

Notes

Wake-up Calls and Warnings

Partners leave wake-up calls and warnings for each other when they really mean they want the other to change. Everyone has effective and ineffective ways to request or refuse change; mostly, however, partners get into power struggles over who is in control and who sets the standards. Sometimes, it is hard to realize your attempts to make things better are ineffective. Successful couples talk about the tough issues, face themselves, their expectations and behavior, and realize when they don't live up to their own standards. This makes for *productive anxiety*. Productive anxiety allows personal growth and relational sexual development. Unproductive anxiety allows you to blame your partner for whatever goes wrong, and fail to claim your part in creating your own displeasure. However, couples who easily discuss other topics may feel hesitant to talk about sex, especially when it is not going well.

A wake up call or warning becomes self-defeating when you ignore it. Objectionable behavior does not disappear by itself even though blaming your partner is easier than claiming your contribution to circumstances you do not like. If your partner is complaining about you, you are getting a warning. If you are complaining about him, you are giving one. Silence and turning away are warnings, too.

Your response to warnings reflects your level of maturity and the meaning of your relationship to you. Does your relationship allow for uncomfortable growth behavior? Do you show your partner the aspects of you that you wish you did not have? Is the purpose of your relationship convenience, money, meals, laundry, reassurance? Do you want to spend the rest of your life in this relationship?

There are numerous variations of wake-up calls, too many to list here; however, items on the following list happen occasionally in every relationship. What you do with them keeps you stale or grows you up. For more information about wake-up calls, read

Why Marriages Succeed or Fail and *Permanent Partners* (see Suggested Readings, page 103).

Suggestions:

1. Read the list and check each characteristic you believe is yours.

2. Next, note each characteristic you see in your partner.

3. Compare your responses. Note how easily or reluctantly you contain your rebuttal. Note whether you focus on your partner or yourself, then focus on yourself.

4. When you are brave and honest enough to tell each other about your shame or self-defeating behaviors, note how you receive the information.

5. Don't explode, don't cave in, and don't leave. Just quiet yourself.

6. Afterwards, talk about what it was like to discuss your respective wake-up calls and warnings.

Wake-up Calls and Warnings

Lack of Contact:

☐ Little or no time for each other.

☐ Little or no affectionate or sexual touching.

☐ Spending more hours alone than together, with one partner dissatisfied with this arrangement.

☐ Longing for (or ignoring) an emotional connection with him while spending time with someone else.

☐ Few conversations, relaxation, or projects together.

☐ Filling time with internet activities (sex, games, chat rooms, etc.) without him.

☐ Perceiving sex as a bore, a chore, time-consuming, anxiety-provoking, or non-existent.

☐ Being distant or aloof.

☐ Arguing, defending, criticizing.

☐ Joining in your partner's arguing, defending, criticizing.

☐ Attacking as a way to relate, especially when stressed, hurt, angry, disappointed, frustrated, etc.

☐ Blaming or shaming yourself or your partner.

☐ Escalating negativity and/or ignoring positives.

☐ Giving or receiving a silent treatment.

□ Ignoring what you hear or know needs to change.

□ Weak confrontation or passive revenge toward your partner's passivity.

□ Withdrawing as a way to relate.

□ Complaining, threatening, or whining.

□ Feeling helpless; believing effective contact depends on the other person.

Lack of Good Will:

☐ Expressing or feeling contempt.

☐ Tolerating contempt instead of dealing with it.

☐ Sarcastic, scathing, nasty, or mean talking.

☐ Victimizing or disempowering yourself or him.

☐ Lying to others.

☐ Excusing your partner's lies.

☐ Hostile teasing.

☐ Pretending his/your hostile teasing doesn't hurt.

☐ Any physical injury, accidental or intentional.

☐ Tolerating punishment of any kind, emotional, mental, and physical.

☐ Demeaning and/or violating your partner.

☐ Behaving dishonestly, lying to yourself about it.

☐ No remorse for obvious or subtle transgressions.

☐ Pretending you don't know what is dishonest or rejecting, excusing or overlooking this "to keep the peace."

☐ Stifling your opinions to avoid unpleasantness.

☐ Accepting your partner's conflict-avoiding agreement.

☐ Overworking, overspending, overeating, gambling, using alcohol and drugs, other behaviors that hurt.

☐ Weak confrontation of transgressions.

☐ Secrets about porn, masturbation, affairs, money, etc.

☐ Tolerating your own or his explosions, caving in, spacing out, numbing, leaving.

Hints for Managing Wake-Up Calls

You can ask your partner to change a behavior but not an experience. Experience is not negotiable.

Accept your own and his right to disagree and remain in relationship, in the same room, at the same time, managing, supporting, and soothing *yourself.*

No matter who does what, neither partner is innocent.

Focus on yourself and express your own experience.

Losing control habitually or automatically does not excuse you from responsibility to contain yourself.

Act with increasing kindness and compassion, not less.

Do this even when your partner does not cooperate.

When you have a choice, always choose integrity, self-respect, and good will ahead of comfort and security.

Tolerate your partner's growth.

Claim your own part in creating your relationship even though you feel awkward and embarrassed.

Manage the monumental challenge that comes with getting what you yearn for.

Notes

Characteristics of Sexually Alive Couples

Satisfied, sexually alive couples have described the qualities that promote long term sexual energy in their relationships. In the next exercise, you can weigh your own positive qualities against known success.

The developmental quality of "emotional maturity" is often an overlooked "given." Nonetheless, level of maturity is a necessary starting place. Maturity is the ability to:

- Define who you are in relationship to another.
- Oversee your own anxiety, insecurity, and needs.
- Admit you are wrong when you are wrong.
- Validate your own feelings and values.
- Manage conflict and grow from those discoveries.
- Observe, soothe, and regulate your own responses.
- Stay connected to your partner, faithful to yourself.
- Verify yourself as whole, separate, and related.
- Honor your agreements and obligations.
- Do all these without exploding, caving in, or leaving.

You can clarify with your partner your requirements for being and becoming more sexually alive. Consider how much and which qualities in this exercise are your strengths and which you would like to build.

Erotic energy is fostered by balancing separateness and togetherness, by honoring your differences, differentness, and similarities. Consider whether your relationship thrives best with sexual exclusivity, a variety of extra-relational, mutual, or private sexual partners, or a combination, and what this means to your relationship. Man-to-man, you have the privilege of *knowingly* including or excluding other partners from your relationship. With secrecy, however, you usurp his choice and endanger his life. Secrecy is not a privilege but a transgression that interferes with your integrity.

33

Ideally, sexually alive couples speak their truth with compassion. They share both trust and hard feelings; yet, positive feelings outweigh negative ones. Mature couples make room for growth, tolerate the results of that growth, and most of all, enjoy each other. Their good will and respect are evident, especially when they disagree. Being in their company feels like a privilege.

Suggestions:

1. Discuss the qualities of sexually alive couples.

2. Consider each quality on the list, and how this is, or is not, part of your own relational repertoire. Then, discuss having your heart's desire.

3. If you think you are in a dead relationship, focus on your own deadness, your part in diminishing yourself and your relation-ship.

4. Don't explode, don't cave in, and don't leave. Just quiet yourself.

5. Discuss what it was like for you to talk about the qualities that keep (or might keep) your relationship sexually alive and happily active.

Characteristics of Sexually Alive Couples

☐ Sense of humor.

☐ More joy, play, and laughter than resentment.

☐ Respect for yourself and your partner.

☐ Frequent affectionate and sexual touch.

☐ Emotional, mental, and physical presence.

☐ Predictability, comfort, familiarity (closeness).

☐ Unpredictability, anxiety, depth (intimacy).

☐ Emotional separateness *and* togetherness.

☐ Self-validation, self-soothing, self-awareness, autonomy, responsible dependency (maturity).

☐ Bringing the whole of who you are to your relationship (integrity).

Notes

Productive Disclosure

A difficult conversation for couples is the one in which they say what is not happening sexually, especially if they feel frustrated or disappointed. "I don't want to hurt your feelings." "I don't want to push you away." "I'm afraid of your silent treatment (anger, guilt, withdrawal, etc.)." "It isn't your fault." Partners often protect each other from feelings and the real meaning of withholding.

Not talking about your experience with your partner walls you off from each other. Talking about your experience removes walls, although initially the closeness can feel threatening. Standing without your partner's support is not easy when you are used to leaning on him (or his wall). When you hold your own, he may feel, for example, rejected, unneeded, or relieved. Protecting your partner from feelings demeans him. Yet, spilling feelings as if they were in charge of you instead of you in charge of them, demeans you.

Willingness to be fully present with your partner can feel risky, but it is crucial to good sex. Erotic sex is not simply intense genital stimulation. It is a balance between anxiety, arousal, and profound connection to yourself in the presence of your partner. Erotic sex happens *with* emotional as well as physical presence. Emotional presence requires, in addition, active self-respect.

Self-respect is an agreement with yourself to be your full self with him, to speak what is important for you. When you give voice to your own experience instead of depending on or judging his, your compassion guides you to debate difficult topics without blame. You can listen without feeling devastated or even getting your feelings bruised. In any case, emotional bruises heal quickly when you're a self-respecting adult in charge of yourself.

When either of you reveals yourself, you are getting or giving a gift of knowing, whether or not you elect to use it. You can use what you know in the service of your own self-respect without exploding, caving in, or leaving. Sexual intimacy can advance with, at the least, verbal, physical, and emotional contact.

You have integrity when you are fully yourself with your partner, that is, open to him and yourself, simultaneously. Intimacy, like integrity, can be unilateral, one person at a time. However, when partners experience it at the same time, it is, indeed, memorable.

Suggestions:

1. Fill out the Disclosure Checklist by yourself.

2. Compare and discuss what you have written.

3. Don't explode, don't cave in, and don't leave. Just quiet yourself.

4. When you have talked as much as you are going to, discuss what talking about disclosures was like.

Productive Disclosure

1. When I feel anxious about being sexual with you, I:

2. Sometimes your touch feels:

3. I'm supposed to like everything we do sexually, but:

4. I truly love how you touch me when you:

5. I feel something special during sex when I:

6. When I feel "careful" during sex, I:

7. I wish I would change the way I:

8. If you could enjoy me more, I might:

9. If I could enjoy me more, I might:

10. If I could enjoy you more, I might:

11. Sex is _____ right now; I wish I could:

12. What I want from you outside of bed is:

13. I can tell when your body is with me and your spirit is off in a sexual fantasy, when:

14. At times, I would like to get more primitive and lusty, and instead, I:

15. At times, I would like to get less primitive and more romantic, and instead, I:

16. I'm afraid you will/won't tell me your dislikes sexually, since:

17. If I tell you I dislike something, you might:

18. Sex is/isn't fun for me, and:

19. I sometimes pretend:

20. When I get the nerve I will:

Sexual Scripts

Each of us learns as a child how to behave in order to be accepted by families, peers, and society. Boys receive both affirmative and negative spoken and unspoken ideas about how to think, feel, and behave. Boys might even receive *different* messages from each parent about the *same* behavior. Parents, teachers, and other adults offer both unintended and purposeful rules about whatever they value. Their guidance about male sexuality can be confusing, especially because heterosexual development is assumed, at least during childhood. Unspoken rules indicate clearly when the topic of sex is off limits and when being gay is even less acceptable. Thus, men grow up with patently unclear, often distorted information.

Children learn "sexual scripts," subconscious prescriptions for how and how not to be sexual, as though you have a script for how to behave, think, or feel. Some scripts are self-defeating. Beneath the surface of human consciousness, we all carry scripts about sex. Thus, becoming more conscious of your sexual script can enhance your relationship.

Uncovering your particular script and using the information on behalf of personal and relational development is a lifelong task. Scripts, by definition, are subconscious. However, you can uncover them by paying close attention to your behavior, thoughts, and feelings, asking yourself relevant questions. This is self-observation in the service of changing your script to fit who you are right now, not who someone else wanted you to be. Self-observation and the resulting increase in awareness expands your options for sexual development under your own, not someone else's, conscious control.

The next exercise can enhance self-observation. If you come upon a blind spot, ask your partner for help, guess, or make up a response. If you don't know which of your ideas and values you received as a child, think about your present values. Did they come from other children, parents, teachers, mentors, abusers? Are they the result of co-operation or resistance? Are they values that do or do not now fit?

Suggestions:

1. Privately, write or ponder your responses to the Sexual Script items.

2. Make enough time together to consider all of your responses. This information, while not secret, is private and vulnerable, so respect all disclosures. Listen attentively without trying to fix him, and keep the information in confidence for life.

3. Don't explode, don't cave in, and don't leave. Just quiet yourself.

4. When you have shared as much as you're going to, discuss what talking about sexual scripts was like.

Sexual Script

1. Write a positive idea you received from your mother (or surrogate) about sexuality:

2. Write a positive idea you received from your father (or surrogate) about sexuality:

3. Write a negative idea you received from your mother (or surrogate) about sexuality:

4. Write a negative idea you received from your father (or surrogate) about sexuality:

5. How might your father describe your body?

6. How might your mother describe your body?

7. How does this affect how you feel about yourself, *now*?

8. How do the ideas in statements 1-6 affect your present behavior?

9. If you could change anything about your present sexual (or lack of sexual) experience, how do you imagine yourself behaving differently?

10. What would you like your partner to learn about his own sexuality and behavior toward you?

11. If your partner changes nothing about his behavior, you may have a difficult choice. Would you be willing to risk improving your own experience, anyway?

Internalized Homophobia and Your Script*

Just as people are given ideas in childhood about life and sex, you are also taught, verbally and nonverbally, attitudes about being different. You learn from people who love you and people who torment you. Sometimes these are one and the same. Often they are other children. Even when you feel pride in being different from the mainstream, early family, peer, and social rejection influences you.

One major unacknowledged rule is set by parents who never speak of, or ask about, sexual feelings or orientation when it seems clearly appropriate. As children grow up gay, they believe they are not supposed to talk about who they love. Beyond this rule of silence is the pervasive negativity about being gay that permeates most friendships, homes, religions, social, government, and political groups.

Men are socialized in western culture to hate and fear homosexual feelings. Homophobia is the fear, loathing, or avoidance of gay people. Internalized homophobia is the fear, shame, and self-hatred that lurks in gay people. This is the result of consistent, impersonal, social *abuse of sexuality*. Thus, shame, fear, and self-hate for a body that does not function according to heterosexual norms occur in many gay men. The abuse of *sexuality* usually goes unrecognized. In subtle and insidious ways, it keeps gay men and lesbians from challenging heterosexism (the assumption straight people make that everyone is heterosexual and that heterosexuality is inherently superior to homosexuality).

While there are certain advantages to growing up gay, homosexuality has traditionally been a story of unactualized, disenfranchised, and injured potential. Few people in our culture, gay and otherwise, reach adulthood without some guilt and repression about sexual pleasure. The burden is heavy, especially after the diminishing lust of a new relationship. Internalized homophobia creates complicated, self-loathing scripts for gay men and their partners, and keeps couples from using the correct pronoun in reference to their partners, even when nothing concrete is at stake.

The next exercise may help you uncover hidden internalized homophobia and, consequently, relieve you of that energy drain so you can use the energy to explore options. You may find that your own sexual script is from the wrong drama and must be revised to fit who you are, today.

Suggestions:

1. Privately, write or ponder your responses to the Internalized Homophobia items.

2. Make enough time to discuss both sets of responses.

3. Don't explode, don't cave in, and don't leave. Just quiet yourself.

4. When you have shared as much as you want, discuss what talking about internalized homophobia is like.

Internalized Homophobia

1. Write positive and negative ideas you received from parenting figures about being gay.

2. Write positive and negative ideas you received from your religion, teachers, and peers about being gay.

3. How do these messages affect how you feel about yourself and your sexuality, now?

4. Write or discuss what feels good to you about being gay and out. If you are not out, or not completely out, discuss what you imagine it might be like.

5. Write or discuss what feels uncomfortable to you about being gay and out, or partially out.

6. As accurately as you can, note which of the items you generated in #5 come from inside you rather than from actual discrimination and survival concerns.

7. What do you think, now, about sissy boys and effeminate men? What did your parents, adults, and peers teach you about this?

8. If you could change anything about being gay, what would you change and how do you imagine your life might be different, as a result?

*Exercise designed by Virginia Erhardt, Ph.D., Atlanta, Georgia.
Reprinted with permission.

Perspectives on Sex

Each generation has its own perspective about sexual knowledge, skills, behavior, and experience. Each religion has its own guidelines about sexuality. In addition, each community has perspective and rules, and so does each family. No wonder so many people grow up confused about sex, especially when your orientation does not fit the mold of the dominant culture. Sexuality exists on a continuum with a wide range of possibilities, not just gay, straight, and bisexual. The next exercise gives you another opportunity to uncover beliefs, attitudes, and perspectives about sexuality, and how they affect you in your present relationship.

Although many avenues lead to exploring sexual perspectives, we will consider here the conventional (usual) and unconventional (unusual). In our culture, the conventional perspective directs us toward dependency and security. It is driven by the popular media in songs, books, and films where we hear: "I'll love you and take care of you (so you won't grow up and leave me)," "You're nobody 'till somebody loves you," "Don't leave me, baby," and, "You made me love you," as though you have no self-direction and are dependent on someone else's love and validation for your survival. The message has you eating when your partner is hungry, sleeping when he is sleepy, having sex when he is horny because you believe you should take care of his needs (and vice versa). Trouble brews when one wants growth (i.e., attend your own needs instead of expecting your partner to do it for you), and the other wants things to stay the same (i.e., keep taking care of each other).

The unconventional viewpoint is based on maturity, self-respect, integrity, and the idea that good, lasting sex happens with fullness, not neediness. This is neither a prevalent nor popular idea. However, with a clear intent to stay together as lovers, yet separate as individuals, you can create hotter sex than behaving as if you were co-dependent or symbiotic. For example, a mature man can comfort himself instead of expecting his partner's reassurance, though he may want and like it. He does not need his partner, he desires him. Paradoxically, self-sufficiency, self-respect, and being separate as individuals helps partners bond more deeply, intimately, and erotically, not less. In our culture, mature love with hot sex is actually *unconventional*! Integrity (wholeness) and individuality can be profoundly effective and lasting aphrodisiacs for partners whether they are in sexually exclusive or sexually inclusive relationships.

Suggestions:

1. Find time to do this exercise together. Read both concepts and discuss what each one means to you, individually and relationally.

2. As you discuss each concept, note where your thoughts diverge. Note whether you feel emotionally separate from your partner's moods, opinions, and needs, or emotionally dependent on them (i.e., his needs guide your behavior more than your own needs do).

3. Don't explode, don't cave in, and don't leave. Just quiet yourself.

4. When you have shared as much as you can for now, take a bit more time to discuss what talking about your different sexual perspectives was like.

Perspectives on Sex

Conventional Perspective

☐ Sex is a natural hunger that comes with puberty.

☐ Focus is mostly on genitals, techniques, and positions, (mostly your partner's).

☐ Good sex means you tune in to your own sensations and have an erotic fantasy, using your partner's touch.

☐ Desire means need and eagerness for sexual behavior.

☐ Desire is a function of needing sex.

☐ Major goals are reducing anxiety, staying comfortable, and relaxing.

☐ Orgasms occur at low levels of arousal.

☐ Silence and conflict-avoidance helps keep peace.

☐ Partner should validate, assure, and protect you.

☐ Security depends on his behavior and opinions.

☐ Emotional security is more important than integrity.

☐ The main complaint is, "I'm not getting what I want from my partner in this relationship."

□ Although reproductive sex is natural, erotic sex is learned, and it happens out of fullness, not need.

□ Focus is mostly on intimate connection and erotic possibilities physically, emotionally, spiritually.

□ Good sex means you tune in your partner *and* your own sensations; arousal is not fantasy-dependent.

□ Desire means eagerness and attraction *for your partner*, before, during, and after orgasm.

□ Desire is a function of want, not need.

□ Sex is not goal oriented, but rather, to give and receive pleasure while you manage your own tension.

□ Orgasms are often with profound arousal and tension.

□ Talking about problems and conflicts is the norm.

□ You reassure and comfort yourself, create your own feelings of safety and security.

□ Feeling secure depends on self-soothing, self-respect, self-validation, and personal responsibility.

□ The main complaint: . ↙ ɪɪɪ not getting what I want from myself in this relationship."

Conversations about Sex

Most committed couples have an experience early in relationship of having sex for hours, revealing all, and believing they will always feel in love. Most trust their attraction to erase all obstacles, now and later.

Partners, subsequently, learn to know each other better as they spend time together, which often means disappointment, frustration, and disillusion. Couples who remain satisfied with each other the way they were when the relationship was young, often find little room for developing and maturing, sexually or otherwise. The power struggle stage is a normal part of growing up in relationship; however, with some couples it lasts the duration of the relationship. Hopefully, the discontent inherent in a power struggle will result in personal growth. That is, with maturity, instead of trying to whip your partner into shape, you take on the job of improving and enriching yourself.

Even men who communicate with ease do not always talk effectively about sex in their relationship, or about what being sexual means. Focusing exclusively on work, finances, or families, to the exclusion of sex and having fun together, makes for dull living.

Men in our culture believe they are supposed to know about sex. In addition, men are shamed into hiding naivete rather than discussing vulnerable topics and asking for help. Discussing sexual pleasures, hopes, and turn-ons can offer you a deeper knowing of yourself and your partner.

The next exercise proposes that you re-experience each other through having structured conversations about sex. You can have similar conversations about money, family, work, home, and whatever else calls for attention. Even if doing the exercise feels contrived and unnatural at first, stay with it until you can talk about something uncomfortable. The discomfort may not leave you, but it need not deter you, either.

53

Suggestions:

1. Make time to be together for this exercise. Write your responses or talk about each statement as you read it.

2. Take turns talking about each statement. Note whether this is easy, difficult, fun, boring, effective, or a waste of time.

3. Don't explode, don't cave in, and don't leave. Just quiet yourself. Stay present and if you feel anxious, manage it and keep talking.

4. When you have finished responding to each other's ideas, notice whether you agree on the meaning of "sexually exclusive," how you might handle "slips," and how you feel talking about it.

Conversations about Sex

1. What I appreciate you for sexually in this relationship is:

2. One of the qualities I love most about you is:

3. For me, sexual exclusivity means:

4. Your attitude about sexual exclusivity, to me, means:

5. The real measure of our loyalty and commitment is:

6. One of the toughest times for me in the sexual aspect of our relationship was/is:

7. What I learned from that about myself:

8. If I had a year left to live, I would:

9. If you had a year left to live, I would:

10. I depend on you for:

11. I think sexual fantasies affect our intimate connection by:

12. When we first got together sexually, I:

13. My hope for the future is:

14. I feel most open and willing to have a sexually revealing conversation with you when I:

15. What I feel (think/want) sexually, now, is:

16. If one of us decides to shift from being sexually exclusive or not exclusive, here's how I want us to deal with it:

17. As limerence fades and we revisit our agreements about sexual behavior, what still works for us and what needs changing, is:

Dysfunctional Sex, Functional Sex, and Erotic Sex

The conventional view of sex includes only two categories, abnormal (dysfunctional) and normal (functional); it works or it doesn't. Unfortunately, we rarely acknowledge sex that is more than just functional. We mostly ignore erotic sex, that is, sex without fantasy, with connection, productive anxiety, and personal and relational depth. Unlike the literature on genital techniques, we do not yet have teaching materials based on the study of sexual *quality*, *experience*, or *meaning*. Although partners can often describe their experience and the meaning of their sexual behavior, we overlook this.

Hot sex happens in many long term male relationships, sometimes extra-relationally. Whether this is useful depends on what sex means to each partner. Sexual exclusivity for male couples need be neither a moral issue nor a measure of fidelity. However, using sex in or out of the relationship to *avoid* relationship issues does not foster maturity or its rewards: erotic sex with a permanent partner.

Couples can stagnate sexually, avoid sex altogether, and/or try to juice up their sex lives with new partners, pornography, and sex toys (which help until they get boring, too). Boredom and monotony are an invitation to change when either man is willing to risk growth toward sexual potential and erotic sex.

What kind of sex is not eventually monotonous? Even one-night-stands get old. Sex with your own partner can, if you allow it, fill you simultaneously with joy and fear, desire and anxiety, appreciation and dread. This kind of sex means you must tolerate rejection, performance anxiety, disapproval, shame, and impermanence, at the same time you soothe yourself, feel deeply committed, loving, and scared. Changing sexual attitudes through self-observation, and renewing yourself in your relationship, makes for sex (and life) that might be nerve-racking, but never monotonous.

You and he already know how to relieve each other's arousal by being intensely genital. Notice which is the hotter fuel for your own sexual behavior, intimacy or horniness. Can you describe the differences? What makes intimacy more (or less) erotic than horniness? Can you capitalize on your differentness and your differences about this?

The capacity for intimacy depends on maturity (the capacity to take care of yourself, to be separate and different in relationship to another), and maturity fuels eroticism, your emotional development, and willingness to embrace growth with your partner.

Suggestions:

1. Make time to read this exercise together. Discuss each statement and compare responses.

2. You may resonate with the information that follows if you stay open to self-observation.

3. Don't explode, don't cave in, and don't leave. Just quiet yourself.

4. When you have finished the exercise, discuss what talking about dysfunctional, functional, and erotic sex felt like.

Dysfunctional Sex

☐ Chemistry is missing at all times.

☐ Arousal is incomplete, absent, or fantasy-dependent.

☐ Orgasms are absent, weak, or fantasy-dependent.

☐ Physical response is occasionally or always insufficient.

☐ Desire for partner is low or absent.

☐ One or both partners are disillusioned and disinterested.

☐ The problem is seen as "belonging" to one partner.

☐ A problem maintains the status of the relationship.

☐ Signals for change are ignored or misinterpreted.

☐ Sexual energy feels threatening to safety and security.

☐ Anxiety is not tolerable to either partner.

☐ Each partner wants the other to provide comfort and protection
from anxiety.

Functional Sex

☐ Chemistry is boring and mediocre, except on vacation.

☐ Arousal is utilitarian, dutiful, or fantasy-dependent.

☐ Orgasms are usually fantasy-dependent or with low levels of arousal.

☐ Physical response is sufficient but without passion.

☐ Desire is for behavior and is mostly opportunistic.

☐ Partners are increasingly disinterested, but do it.

☐ No problem is noticed except monotony and low arousal.

☐ Comfort maintains the status of the relationship.

☐ Neither wants to risk the consequences of change.

☐ Sexual energy is acceptable, within certain limits.

☐ Anxiety is not well tolerated by either partner.

☐ Each partner comforts and validates the other to protect each from anxiety and risk.

Erotic Sex

☐ Chemistry is almost always present and changing.

☐ Arousal is often erotic, fantasy is not needed; partners arouse each other without it.

☐ Orgasms are intense, often occur with high arousal.

☐ Physical response is intact and often passionate.

☐ Desire is for partner, not for release.

☐ Partners increasingly interest each other.

☐ Problems have meaning and potential for growth.

☐ Discomfort signals growth and shifts the status of the relationship to a higher level of sexual functioning.

☐ One or both risk, tolerate, and appreciate change.

☐ Sexual energy increases as partners develop in maturity and integrity with each other.

☐ Anxiety is tolerated and used for erotic growth.

☐ Each partner soothes his own anxiety and tolerates the other's.

For more information, see David Schnarch's *Passionate Marriage* in Suggested Readings section.

Ranking Sexual Behavior

1. Choose five or more sexual behaviors you engage in, or wish to engage in, and list them from most to least preferred.

2. List all sexual behaviors you and your partner now engage in, from the most to the least frequent.

3. Compare your first with your second list, then compare your lists with his.

Closeness and Intimacy

For some men, there seems to be an inverse relationship between being best friends and being sexually attracted to each other. Best friends not only care about each other, they know each other so well they can often predict the other's thoughts, feelings, and behavior. The foundation of their relationship is based on friendship and closeness, not sex. Best friends generate familiar, comfortable, safe, stable, and predictable feelings. Committed couples have large quantities of this kind of closeness, it makes relationships flourish. However, for sexual energy to flourish, the familiar must occasionally touch something new; comfort must become invigorated with something risky; and predictability must undergo a dash of surprise.

Intimacy is different from closeness. Intimacy involves novel, strange, uncomfortable, and unpredictable experience. The very nature of intimacy keeps you on your toes, awake and new to yourself, and therefore, new to your partner. Intimacy brings balance to stability and familiarity. While closeness allows you to know your partner better, intimacy allows you to know *yourself* better. Intimacy helps couples bring exciting and genuinely new energy to their relationship. To risk this excitement means you feel whole, genuine, authentic, and unafraid to be with your lover in this way.

Genuineness and authenticity, in contrast to sexual fantasy, is a characteristic of integrity. It is a profound, erotic turn-on to push your own emotional frontier. But, genuine energy can be frightening if you fear merging with your partner and losing yourself as a whole, intact, and separate person. Tuning in to a fantasy instead of to your partner is a shield that avoids merger fear. On the other hand, knowing your own boundaries, that is, knowing yourself as a separate person, allows you to merge sexually, at will, knowing for certain you will emerge intact and whole.

Integrity is a lifelong aphrodisiac. Strangeness, differentness, depth, surprise, and unpredictability increase sexual energy. This is a new perspective. Being deeply in touch with your separate nature and sharing that with your partner, intensifies intimacy. Being in bed with the man you love, who, at the moment, is strange, new, and unpredictable, is stimulating when you risk the unknown.

When you are most intimate, you are most deeply, profoundly connected to yourself. That is when you feel the most intense toward your partner. Mature couples know how to move back and forth between closeness and intimacy, that is, between feeling safe and risking new behavior, between comfort and anxiety, between the predictable and the unknown, and transform that anxiety into erotic sex. That is *productive* anxiety.

Managing productive anxiety invites intimacy. We often confuse closeness with intimacy. Understanding this basic yet complicated difference can increase your experience of familiarity, safety, comfort, and predictability, and deepen your experience of strangeness, unpredictability, depth. Both are necessary for sexual aliveness.

Suggestions:

1. Find time to read the next page together. Discuss how the shift in thinking suits you or does not fit.

2. For more information, read *The Art of Intimacy* or *Windows of Experience* (Suggested Readings, page 103).

3. Don't blow up, don't cave in, and don't leave. Just quiet yourself.

4. Talk about what it was like to consider new perspectives about closeness and intimacy.

Closeness is . . .

- Familiar, comfortable, and predictable.

- Affirming and sustaining each other.

- Partners validating and supporting each other.

- When your partner is slightly more important to you than you are to yourself.

- Experiencing your partner in shared space.

- Intense interpersonal awareness of your relationship to your partner.

- Partners caring for and complementing each other.

- Gladly giving up portions of personal space and options to know your partner more deeply.

- Negotiable because it is mostly about behavior and comfort, both of which are negotiable.

- Knowing your partner.

Intimacy is . . .

- Unfamiliar, risky, surprising, often uncomfortable.

- Affirming and sustaining yourself.

- Self-validating, self-affirming, self-supporting, self-respectful.

- Being yourself without stopping your partner from being who he is; accepting him as he is.

- Relinquishing no part of yourself to bond with your partner even though dependency happens.

- Experiencing yourself, deeply, in the presence of your partner, not necessarily simultaneously.

- Being willing to grow and change individually, and tolerate the anxiety that accompanies growth.

- Choosing to be compassionately truthful with yourself and your partner, in relationship, physically near each other.

- Not negotiable, even though it is often difficult to be fully you with the person you love and depend on.

- Knowing yourself.

Purposeful Sexual Partnerships

The key word in this exercise is "purposeful." The purpose, however, is not to get your partner to be the man with whom you thought you were in relationship. Your task is to accept your partner as he is.

That leaves the changing to you. The purpose of this exercise is for you to notice the kind of person you want to be, in relationship with him. "But I can't be the kind of partner I want to be until my partner is how he should be." This stance cheats you of being in charge of yourself. As an adult, you already are the person you choose to be. You can do this with compassion, rebellion, or passivity, but neither permission, approval, nor objection from your partner can change who you already are. Only you can make that change.

The next exercise offers another glimpse at how you can be the partner you want to be, or more of the partner you already are. You can intensify your sexual relationship by developing to the point where you like who you are with your partner.

The following statements in support of purposeful sexual partnerships have five options. You are invited to decide whether you are:

never, rarely, sometimes, frequently, always

the way the item indicates. You may dislike some of the statements, but it is important to consider all of them. This means you are willing to observe your own behavior as well as your partner's, hear what your partner has to say about yours, and speak your truth with compassion.

Suggestions:

1. Fill out the exercise privately, on your own. Then, compare your answers. Listen closely to each other's responses for each item.

2. Note discrepancies. If you think you do something *always* and your partner disagrees, you are on fertile ground. Your experience of yourself may be different from your partner's experience of you. Observing how you handle discrepancies permits you to see how you react or respond separately and together.

3. Note agreements. Appreciate them and move on; closeness, not intimacy, occurs when people agree or feel the same about an issue. The invitation to erotic energy is in differentness more than in sameness.

4. Don't explode, don't cave in, and don't leave. Just quiet yourself and stay in relationship.

5. When you have finished the exercise, discuss what it was like for you to talk about purposeful sexual partnerships.

Purposeful Sexual Partnerships

1. I listen actively when my partner talks about sex.

   never   rarely   sometimes   frequently   always

2. I say "no" to my partner when I am not interested in sex.

   never   rarely   sometimes   frequently   always

3. I make appointments to express sexual frustration.

   never   rarely   sometimes   frequently   always

4. I engage my partner with sexual enthusiasm and love.

   never   rarely   sometimes   frequently   always

5. I don't criticize, withdraw, or get defensive after sex.

   never   rarely   sometimes   frequently   always

6. I stay present, clear, and manage my own sexual anxiety.

   never   rarely   sometimes   frequently   always

7. I feel connected to myself and my partner before, during, and after sex.

   never   rarely   sometimes   frequently   always

8. When my partner feels emotional about sex, I am present and responsive.

   never   rarely   sometimes   frequently   always

9. When my partner gets on my nerves, especially about sex, we discuss it to completion.

never   rarely   sometimes   frequently   always

10. We engage together in outside interests, projects, ideas, discussions.

never   rarely   sometimes   frequently   always

11. We both have sexual energy for the other.

never   rarely   sometimes   frequently   always

12. Our relationship is enhanced (or harmed) by sexual exclusivity.

never   rarely   sometimes   frequently   always

13. Our relationship is enhanced (or harmed) by including other sex partners.

never   rarely   sometimes   frequently   always

Sexual Style

We don't think much about sexual style as another royal road to the unconscious. Yet, your style is founded on subconscious patterns that repeatedly support, neutralize, or block intimacy and erotic enjoyment. Your sexual style reveals subconscious patterns. Your style is a form of communication with your partner. People almost always find a partner whose sexual style pushes their own growth; you can discover this through the messages in your lovemaking.

Sexual style reflects your connection to yourself as well as your ability to bond without feeling trapped or rejected. Mature men can change styles as circumstances shift. Styles often follow the same patterns in and out of bed. Styles are not right or wrong, just ways people express themselves. Style shows the way you accept or reject opportunities for emotional growth and connection. Awareness of your sexual style can increase your sexual options. Which partner is always the top? Is sex the primary way you connect? What matters most to you, sexually? Are you impulsive, spontaneous, intentional, picky? Does your sexual energy control you? Do you control it?

Since few models for male sexuality exist without a strong focus on genital stimulation, male couples are free to experiment. Traditional, politically correct male sexual relationships can now be observed, understood, revised, or ignored by each couple, according to their own wishes, values, and development.

Like personality, everyone has sexual style. It may or may not mimic personality style. For example, a passive person may be assertive sexually. A dominating person might be shy sexually. More often, however, sexual style follows the same pattern in and out of bed (or wherever you have sex). This means a chronically angry or suspicious person is probably not going to be a generous, sensitive lover; a gentle, considerate person is unlikely to be selfish and demanding in bed.

71

Behavior during the few hours before sex reveals how a pattern begins and what will happen next. For example, invitations for sex are characteristically predictable over time and might include being playful, enthusiastic, hesitant, reserved, funny, assertive, passive, seductive, romantic, leading, expressive, self-confident, teasing, etc. Or it might include being anxious, hostile, mean, tricky, pitiful, fearful, guilty, pleasureless, self-serving, etc. These characteristics are hard to ignore in a partner and easy to overlook in one's self.

The way you approach foreplay and whether you engage in it might suggest how you relate in other areas. For example, fears of shame, punishment, rejection, neglect, and intrusion often inhibit initiating or responding to an invitation (excluding men who sexualize fear and are thus aroused by dominant-submissive or sadistic-masochistic sex). Your expectation of sexual pleasure or pain reveals your outlook about life as much as about sex. Foreplay, then, has subconscious aspects that direct what happens next.

Examples of foreplay style include: giving, receptive, skilled, smooth, lusty, tentative, conventional, imaginative, persistent, reliable, conscientious, dramatic, leisurely, sensitive, aggressive. Styles that usually distance a partner include: indifference, selfishness, caution, carelessness, inhibition, aversion, aloofness. Observing and restructuring your own patterns in the context of your relationship is useful for shifting sex from mediocre to memorable. Foreplay, including behaviors you no longer engage in, holds a message not only about the meaning of sex to you both, but about what you mean to each other. Foreplay is filled with self-discovery.

Although foreplay and intercourse require knowledge and skill, they may also express love, lust, aggression, or indifference to your partner. You are not only using your partner's body to give and get pleasure, you are also communicating with your mind, heart, and, perhaps, soul. Intercourse style might include: loving, endearing, lascivious, spontaneous, erotic, playful, serious, talkative, primitive, adventurous, irreverent, tender, creative, juicy, and soulful feelings. Distancing styles might include: compliant, dutiful, vigilant, intimidating, insistent, coercive, manipulative, disconnecting, abusive. Describe your sexual style with words and listen for the unspoken message you send your lover. Then notice if the same message is also given in nonsexual interactions.

Partners often push each other to grow in directions that feel awkward. This is useful. The results of childhood socialization with love or abuse and everything between, inevitably surface in sexual relationships. This is how committed relationships help you grow into your adult capacity for living fully. Childhood hurts can be managed by purposeful activation of your competent adult self when you feel afraid, ashamed, rejected, violated, and whatever else turns you off (or inappropriately on). As an emotionally competent adult, you can struggle *effectively* with unproductive anxiety.

Your partner either will, or will not, deal with his own anxiety as you observe and change your own sexual patterns. For example, if you space out or require a fantasy for stimulation while you ignore your connection to your partner, and you change this, he may find the new connection weird, different, stimulating, confusing, frightening, loving, or all of these. He will manage his own responses as you behave more authentically.

Being increasingly yourself--authentic--in relationship is how growth occurs. Compromising who you are--your integrity-- does not help you feel secure. Emotional security comes and goes like anything else in life. However, security does not require you to protect your partner from anxiety, give up your sense of yourself, compromise your integrity, or embrace helplessness. Tolerating *productive* anxiety in the service of intimacy will create an emotional environment supportive of deeply erotic, lusty sex, and create more than just physical relief and release. You know your anxiety is productive when you move to a higher level of functioning because of it.

For all styles and behaviors, presence is the most important characteristic. Partner sex without presence is masturbation with a pretense of relationship. If both partners like it that way, it is not a problem until one wants emotional contact. The dissatisfied partner will often attempt to reconnect, at which time the growth cycle can resume.

Suggestions:

1. Brainstorm with your partner to create a list of words that describe your characteristic as well as maverick sexual style. Notice whether you slide into a familiar pattern of acceptance, criticism, blame, or shame around sexual behavior (or lack of it).

2. In separate columns, note how you are alike and how you are different. Talk about how these styles affect your respective sexual energies.

3. Don't explode, don't cave in, and don't leave. Just quiet yourself.

4. Discuss what it was like to talk about sexual style.

List of Words Describing Sexual Style

Mine   Yours

(Use the words you listed on the previous page)

1. The first thing that happens is:

2. And then:

3. Here's how I predictably respond:

4. Here's how you predictably respond:

5. I do my predictable part, anyway, because:

6. If I change the way I respond, then:

7. I would change this if I:

Maturity

Because the term "maturity" has a variety of meanings, designing your own definition will give you words and meanings you both understand. Knowing what emotional maturity means in *your* relationship gives you sexual options. Maturity does not mean boring, grown-up, unsexy behavior; rather, it means you are in charge of your life and responsible for your decisions. For example:

- Maturity is the quality that helps you avoid compliance, defiance, and indecision about sex.

- Maturity helps you tolerate yearning for what you don't have, grants you courage to go for what you want, and gives the freedom to receive it.

- Maturity gives you enough self-support to speak your truth, knowing it will push you to contain yourself, and allows your competence to inhibit the urge to defend, criticize, refute, explode, cave in, give up, or leave.

- Maturity helps you avoid no-growth agreements and accept beneficial change even as it feels emotionally unbearable and you bear it.

- Maturity gives you resources for integrity and self-awareness, both of which are required for effective maintenance of erotic energy.

"Must I have a partner to develop integrity and maturity?"

No, but a partner will push your growth in almost every way you have unknowingly avoided all your life. On the other hand, only you can lead yourself toward your sexual potential. Nobody else can manage your anxiety or choose for you between integrity and emotional comfort.

An efficient definition of maturity, with which by now you are familiar, is: "Don't explode, don't cave in, and don't leave, just quiet yourself." This does not mean you stifle feelings, but rather, you contain them, temporarily. You restrain yourself from interrupting your partner, set aside your rebuttal and listen (especially to his intent) because you want to, not because you have to. You consider his message respectfully and responsibly, especially when you do not like or agree with what you hear. Responsibility is the ability to respond and remain connected to yourself and your partner even while you disagree.

Suggestions:

1. Make time to read and discuss the next statements. Add your own favorite characteristics to the list. Discuss what further development might mean to your self-respect and, thus, your sexual relationship. Restrain yourself from focusing on your partner's development.

2. Don't explode, don't cave in, and don't leave. Just quiet yourself.

3. When you have completed the exercise, talk about how it was to define and explore maturity together.

Maturity Is the Ability to . . .*

☐ Soothe your *own* anxieties, fears, and insecurities.

☐ Maintain your identity in the face of pressure to conform to another person's idea of how you should be.

☐ Tolerate intense feelings, yours and his.

☐ Tolerate risk, contradiction, and ambivalence.

☐ Let feeling dissatisfied promote change, not resentment.

☐ Stand apart as separate people, and value togetherness.

☐ Set your limits with consideration, not responsibility, for your partner's needs, moods, desires. Honor your obligations and agreements.

☐ Enjoy yourself with your partner, and enjoy your partner.

☐ Share the best and the worst of yourself.

☐ Look inside, tolerate what you find, and let him in.

☐ Be of good will in words and actions, even in anger.

☐ Balance yourself when you are pulled off center.

☐ Play together.

*With appreciation to Drs. Murray Bowen, Joen Fagan, David Hawkins, Tom Malone, David Schnarch, John Warkintin, and Carl Whitaker.

Notes

Contradictions

Contradictions and paradoxes are normal, useful, everyday events occurring with individuals and partners. A contradiction is an opposing, contrary, or conflicting opinion or event; a paradox is a statement or idea contrary to popular belief, which can actually be true. Both help people come to terms with separateness.

Contradictions cause conflict and can expand your thinking. Managing conflict is necessary for emotional growth and simple survival. This does not mean stifling your opinions or deferring to keep the peace. Noticing and managing contradiction means you bring together seemingly conflicting ideas, beliefs, and values. To see contradiction from a higher vantage point, you view one side of an argument as a possibility, see the other side as equally plausible, and find a way to bring them together into another, comprehensively different, whole. For couples, this means you stop pointing out the other's errors and make sense of them in context.

The statement, "I want my partner to desire me, but I feel trapped by his desire," is a fertile contradiction that invites self-observation. Is "being desired" tolerable? Who imposes feeling "trapped?" Einstein said that you cannot solve the problem on the level of the problem. This means you rise above the problem to see the whole picture. For this example, feeling trapped is a function of what you tell yourself, not of your partner's wants or behavior. How you see a problem may *be* the problem.

"I want an intimate relationship where I am in control." In sexual relationships, the contradiction is that intimacy and emotional control do not co-exist. Emotional and physical intimacy happens between peers, not between men who control and who (subconsciously) agree to be controlled. Consciously accepting responsibility for yourself removes dependency and control as major issues. "I want an intimate relationship where I am in control *of me*," is a statement of authenticity and possibility. This happens when you accept yourself as an emotionally capable man, separate from your partner. In relationship language, this means you have enough separateness and maturity to value your partner's perspective whether or not you agree with it. Creating choices of "both and" instead of "either or" eliminates power struggles without erasing personal power.

Suggestions:

1. Read the next exercise with your partner. Notice how easy or difficult it is to bring apparent contradictions together. Add your own thoughts to the list.

2. Don't explode, don't cave in, and don't leave. Just quiet yourself.

3. When you have finished the exercise, talk about what it was like to consider your individual and interpersonal contradictions.

Using Contradictions

I want...	And I also want...
To be close.	Solitude.
Self-reliance.	Dependability.
To love unconditionally.	To honor my conditions.
To be deeply desired by my partner.	Freedom from desire and being desired.
To develop by myself.	To develop in relationship.
Self-awareness and autonomy.	Suggestions and guidance.
To live in the moment.	To plan for the future.
Oneness with my partner.	Separateness and individuality.
To work to create a good relationship.	Some rest from all this work on our relationship.
Passion and intensity with my partner.	Friendship and reliability.
Sexual arousal and erotic connection.	Companionable peace and quiet.
I want to do all of this yesterday; life is too short to waste even a moment.	There is time for this; life must be savored slowly, a little at a time.

Notes

84

Thoughts about Sex

The next page is an assortment of ideas shared by sexual couples. They have discovered how to shift from "limerence," the magical, hormone-filled stage of being "in love," to seeing and accepting each other as they actually are, faults and goodness. When romance fades, the reality of love can begin for real. Emotional development often shows itself in ways that look like relationship problems. These problems are actually guideposts in disguise. Problems allow you to develop skills such as presence, self-respect, and self-validation, and then to connect intimately. Growing real (and growing up) in relationship fosters wholeness, which, when seen as an opportunity instead of a problem, deepens the erotic experience and heightens your sense of your sexual self.

Any high-school boy can perform genitally, without a clue about who he is or what sex means except that it feels compelling. Teenagers are mostly dependent people learning how to separate from their parents and become themselves. Dependency is a stage from which most of us evolve only after four or five or more decades of mental and emotional development. Believing your partner is supposed to meet your needs and validate you is one way to keep yourself dependent. When your partner does not give you space to meet your own needs and you do not give it to yourself, resentful dependency heightens, effectively blocking erotic energy for your partner. Giving yourself what you need can transform the testosterone lust of early love into a profoundly erotic, long term, intimate relationship.

Validation is not an *adult* need, it is an interaction which adults should be able to have with themselves. A partner's validation can build trust, comfort, and good will; however, if you *need* it from him, it signals dependency. Maturity builds self-validation and vice versa. Even though it is comforting to be validated by your partner, *self-validation* is the quality required for erotic intimacy.

An increase in self-validation can also happen when you discover the meaning of sex with your partner beyond physical release, *and* when you are willing to support yourself sexually. Sexual meaning adds richness and depth to your relationship, especially your relationship with yourself. Meaning is more than understanding, it is being present to yourself while you are physically with your partner, where you feel the sexual connection and what that means. Such profound knowing can be awfully uncomfortable and wonderfully erotic, which is why self-support is required.

On the other hand, playfulness and sensuality mixed with sexual contact is an expression of joy most deeply felt with a beloved. When you allow play *and* self-support, you build an erotic connection that can last.

Suggestions:

1. Read the next page aloud with your partner. Discuss the notions and their possible influence on you. Add your own wisdom to the collection.

2. Don't explode, don't cave in, and don't leave. Just quiet yourself.

3. When you have finished what you can do for now, discuss what it was like for you to talk about these ideas.

Thoughts about Sex

1. Unlike casual sex and sex in a state of mindless bliss, intimate, erotic sex is developed, over time, between partners who can tolerate profound desire.

2. You deepen your ability to love each time you see the other person clearly and accept who he is apart from your own needs, wants, and beliefs.

3. If you respect yourself, you invite intimacy instead of attachment hunger into your life.

4. In a loving relationship you feel better, not worse, about yourself most of the time.

5. Attention, compassion, conflict, and differentness can each be aphrodisiacs in adult relationships.

6. Not all adults are grown-up enough to put love and sex in the same bed.

7. Intense genital stimulation and arousal are necessary but not sufficient for erotically intimate sex.

8. Compliant and obligatory sex lead to sexual apathy and resentment.

9. Sexual apathy is often an unspoken plea for presence, liveliness, differentness, or change.

10. No matter what the complaint, neither is innocent.

11. Until you can validate yourself, your dependency prohibits erotic sex.

12. You will utilize considerable self-observation to be capable of erotic intimacy.

13. Loving, wanting, and receiving require you to tolerate impermanence and loss.

14. Generosity (lack of possessiveness) is an important characteristic for enduring couples, whether sexual exclusivity or inclusivity symbolizes your commitment.

15. Sexual exclusivity is a vow you make to yourself, not to your partner; it is a personal decision you make in thoughtful discussion with each other, over time.

16. Waning sexual desire is an invitation to explore yourself, not find another sex partner.

17. Declining frequency of sexual behavior does not necessarily mean less satisfaction; in a lively, mature relationship it may indicate fulfillment.

18. In a lifelong relationship, one of you will eventually lose the other. You can choose an intimate relationship and suffer that loss but once.

With appreciation for personal communication over several decades to: Howard M. Halpern, David M. Hawkins, Thomas P. Malone, Andrew Mattison, David M. Schnarch, Stuart Strenger, John Warkentin, & Carl A. Whitaker.

Sexual Potential

Sexual potential is the highest level to which you can take your erotic energy. It includes your capacity to be deeply in touch with yourself mentally, emotionally, physically, and spiritually. This handbook is about stretching toward your sexual potential in a committed relationship, a movement that requires maturity. Maturity is filled with paradox: it requires you to acknowledge and accept yourself and your partner as you are, now, before you can move into a sacred erotic sphere. That is, before you can enrich yourself, you accept yourself. You will recall from previous sections that maturity is, among other things, an ability to soothe yourself, tolerate anxiety, observe and use conflict and contradiction, honor your agreements, and hold fast to your identity when you feel pressure to conform to someone else's needs. This is but the baseline leverage you must have to elevate your personal potential.

We do not yet know if men reach their sexual potential extra-relationally, whether sexual potential is a function of emotional and physical intimacy with one partner, some of each, or something else. Sexual potential is considered an aspect of sacred development, according to certain eastern philosophy. To approach sexual potential, you might determine where and how you stop expressing yourself in good faith, with integrity. Expressing yourself means you intentionally let your partner know you in all your aspects. If you are able to have lusty extra-relational sex, the obstacle is not age, boredom, physical conditions, or medication that holds you back from your own partner. Fortunately, your erotic energy is not about your partner's responses to you, it is your own creation.

"Well, OK, but how does a guy manage his own maturity and sexuality in only one sexual relationship?"

Good question. So far, nobody knows the influence of sexual exclusiveness or inclusiveness on sexual potential for male couples. This is for partners to decide with each other and future researchers to explore. Sexual exclusivity may not even be an issue for mature men in marriages or committed relationships; some men are able to share themselves fully with their own partner and have clear emotional and behavioral boundaries at the same time with other sex partners or shared sex partners. Because sex has different meanings, discovering what it means to you helps you know whether inclusive or exclusive (or a combination) sexual behavior fits for you, whether it creates distance or intimacy, and how you want to manage that in your own relationship.

When you claim responsibility for your own thoughts, body, and soul, including your sexual potential in relationship to a beloved partner, you proclaim yourself mature. Your soul may belong to God, but your conscious decisions belong to you. You have resources with which to revise the thoughts, feelings, and behaviors no longer useful to you. This happens independently of your partner's changes.

Pushing your relationship and sexuality forward can feel risky because you have more to lose than if you have little erotic energy with your partner. Emotional distance minimizes the grief of eventual loss and death, but you suffer more, now, when you sacrifice intimacy for security. Sexual feelings for your partner means you gain a loving, erotic relationship for the duration, however long or brief. Of all people, male couples know intimately the profound devastation an early death brings.

Reaching toward your sexual potential, you experience what happens after you quiet yourself. You move your sexual energy forward and upward, sometimes together, where you can reinvent or discover sacred sex.

Suggestions:

1. Read the next page to yourself. Note which items match your own thinking. Focus on the part of your life for which you can claim complete responsibility. If you realize that your dependency on your partner's behavior interferes with erotic feelings for him, use that as information about your own development, and discuss your responses in terms of your own experience.

2. Don't explode, don't cave in, and don't leave. Just quiet yourself.

3. When you have finished, discuss what it was like to talk about sexual potential.

Notes

Reaching Toward Sexual Potential Includes:

☐ Willingness to be totally yourself, without pretense, including sexually.. (Integrity)

☐ The capacity to be caught off guard and enjoy the surprise and novelty. (Playfulness)

☐ The ability to find fresh possibilities in familiar surroundings. (Creativity)

☐ Occasional longing for the presence and absence of your partner. (Separateness)

☐ The ability to play, be curious, be creative. (Intimacy)

☐ Allowing integrity to override the wounds of bigotry, social injustice, and childhood. (Maturity)

☐ The ability to observe, tolerate, and manage your own anxiety, ambivalence, and contradictions. (Responsibility)

☐ Willingness to risk being sexual in new ways. (Curiosity)

☐ Accepting the unchangeable rhythms and cycles of life. (Surrender)

☐ Acknowledging impermanence and loss, yet loving deeply anyway. (Acceptance)

Notes

94

Practicing Loss

Nobody likes this last exercise. Yet, every gay man has already done it by losing a friend to AIDS. Every couple with an HIV+ partner practices living with loss. The reality of AIDS pushes death and loss into our collective and individual consciousness. Valuing the time left in your and your partner's lives honors those who have already faced so much loss. Emotional maturity moves forward through the realization that life is impermanent and loss is inevitable. Being mindful of life's endings can provide the spark that urges you toward self-awareness, emotional development, and erotic intimacy, *now*.

Being alone is the last stage of every relationship. Practicing loss means planning how your life will evolve without your partner. You can plan for the inevitable or pretend to have unlimited time. Either way has consequences. Although planning for loss is painful, it highlights the preciousness of life. Valuing your partner and your life together are developmental tasks whatever your age, health status, and however much time you think you have left.

If you are over fifty or sixty, consider the next decades and how you want to spend them with your partner. Think about growing older together and what that means to you, and then think about growing old alone, and how you will manage emotionally, socially, and financially. Will you move forward in your own living? Is your support system in place? Do you know where important papers and items are that were the task or charge of your partner?

If you are under fifty, think about what the next years might bring for you if your partner were to die prematurely. How do you see your friends who have lost beloved partners manage? Think about being alone and how you would manage emotionally, socially, and financially. How will you move forward in your own living and loving? Is your support system in place?

If you or your partner is HIV+, how do you decide where you draw the line between what is allowable sexually and what is not? Do you discuss how you want to live the rest of your lives? You can lose your partner once, when he dies, or you can lose him little by little, every day, by loving him less so that his death is not so devastating a loss. For everyone who loves, the inevitable tragedy of love is loss. The gift of life is going after what you want, now, not despite that eventuality but because of it. One might even say that love is foreplay for Death.

Suggestions:

1. Read the next page and do the exercise alone. Then, read aloud to each other what you have written.

2. Discuss responses to your own experience of planning for loss, and what losing your partner means to you.

3. Don't explode, don't cave in, and don't leave. Just quiet yourself.

4. When you have finished, talk about how it was for you to think about death and practicing loss.

Practicing Loss

1. Collect your thoughts about your partner and what losing him means to you. Write that here.

2. Create an epitaph for your partner: a few words for his grave-stone that express your experience of him.

3. Write a short note to your (live) partner. Include appreciations, resentments, and regrets, in that order, about your present and your history together.

Notes

98

Closing Comments

Numerous sex how-to books teach technical skills, but few highlight presence or anxiety tolerance, let alone *sacred* pleasure. Books and videos on Tantra come closest.

Sacred pleasures, the spiritual aspect of connecting with your beloved through erotic sex, is the direction toward which these exercises point. Yet, the map for this journey is your own consciousness. Many, if not all, intimate moments are sacred. In sacred space, words are acceptable but not necessary. A simultaneous deep connection to yourself, your partner, and a higher power is sacred, no matter in which order these experiences happen. "Down and dirty" behavior may seem profane, but it, too, takes place in sacred space. Sacredness, like beauty, is in the eye, or soul, of the beholder. The soul speaks so softly that to hear it, we must listen with exquisite presence.

We continue to collect information and would appreciate your comments and your response on the anonymous survey in the back of this handbook. Your input is valuable to ongoing research.

May the rest of your journey proceed with integrity, love, laughter, and relationship as a guide to living gloriously.

Notes:

About the Author

How, you might ask, does a grandmother offer sexual advice to male couples? And, why? Several responses come immediately to mind. In the first place, I think the planet would be better off with more love than we presently exhibit. Surely, we need sex expressed with love instead of need, relief, duty, indifference, coercion, or abuse. From personal experience, clinical practice, and research, I am convinced that maturity and integrity help us love more effectively than does communication and reciprocity, although the latter are important. Presently, the culture (the *entire* culture) overlooks maturity and integrity as vital to long term sexual relationships. Co-dependency gives couples little authenticity or freedom to connect erotic sex with mature love.

In the second place, the few (hidden) gay men in my own family were some of the most loving people of my childhood. Their survival, personal and professional, depended on secrecy, so I learned quickly not to ask questions. I saw the pain that accompanies denial of self ("selficide") only many decades later, with friends and colleagues who had narrowly escaped their own childhood horrors. I learned early that pretense and secrets wound souls even as they preserve lives. This was brought close to home by relatives who survived (and others who succumbed later) to the holocaust of WWII.

In the third place, why *not* me? As a clinical psychologist, clinical nurse specialist, sex therapist, and workshop leader for almost three decades, I have seen many hundreds of heterosexual, lesbian, and gay couples, foreign and domestic, of color and ethnic diversity. I thank them, now, for their patience and apologize for my ignorance. Mostly, I have felt a deep appreciation for how they demonstrate *being related*. Occasionally, I have felt ashamed of my own unexpunged, hidden prejudice. It seems only fair that I give back, here, some of what I have learned.

I have been in the independent practice of psychotherapy and sex therapy in Atlanta, Georgia since 1976. I have worked with individuals, couples, and groups for a quarter of a century, and designed the *Journey Toward Intimacy: A Retreat for Couples* weekend sexuality workshops for couples of all lifestyles.

I have published dozens of professional and lay articles and chapters, the four handbooks with a fifth (couples with disabilities) under consideration. I led Sexual Attitude Reassessment programs and various other sexuality workshops and training seminars in this country and abroad for two decades.

Before I am too old to drive, I shall take time to follow my desires in a small motor home. Honk if you see me.

Jeanne Shaw, Ph.D.
1998

Suggested Readings

Anand, Margo. (1989). *The Art of Sexual Ecstasy: The Path of Sacred Sexuality for Western Lovers.* Los Angeles: Jeremy P. Tarcher, Inc.

Baird, Robert M., & Rosenbaum, Stuart, E. (Eds.). (1998). *Same Sex Marriage: The Moral and Legal Debate.* Amherst, NY: Prometheus.

Berzon, Betty. (1988). *Permanent Partners: Building Gay and Lesbian Relationships that Last.* NY: E. P. Dutton.

Berzon, Betty. (1996). *The Intimacy Dance: A Guide to Long Term Success in Gay and Lesbian Relationships.* NY: E. P. Dutton.

Clark, Don. (1977). *Loving Someone Gay.* Millbrae, CA: Celestial Arts.

Gottman, John. (1995). *Why Marriages Succeed or Fail.* NY: Simon & Schuster.

Isay, Richard A. (1989). *Being Homosexual: Gay Men and Their Development.* NY: Avon.

Kramer, Joseph. (1992). *Fire on the Mountain: An Intimate Guide to Male Genital Massage.* Oakland, CA: Erospirit Research Institute. Video, 45 mins.

Malone, Thomas P., & Malone, Patrick T. (1987). *The Art of Intimacy.* NY: Prentice Hall.

Malone, Patrick T., & Malone, Thomas P. (1992). *The Windows of Experience.* NY: Simon & Schuster.

McWhirter, David P., & Mattison, Andrew M. (1984). *The Male Couple: How Relationships Develop*. Englewood Cliffs, NJ: Prentice-Hall, Inc.

Morganthaler, John, & Joy, Dan. (1994). *Better Sex Through Chemistry*. Petaluma, CA: Smart Publications.

Rotello, Gabriel. (1997). *Sexual Ecology: AIDS and the Destiny of Gay Men*. NY: Dutton.

Schnarch, David. (1997). *Passionate Marriage: Sex, Love, and Intimacy in Emotionally Committed Relationships*. NY: W. W. Norton.

Community Resources

American Academy of Psychotherapists
P.O. Box 1611
New Bern, NC 28563

    Phone: 919-634-3066
    Fax: 919-634-3067
    Email: aapoffice@aol.com

American Association of Sex Educators, Counselors, and Therapists
(AASECT)
P.O. Box 238
Mount Vernon, IA 52314

    Phone: 319-895-8407
    Fax: 319-895-6203

The Society for the Scientific Study of Sexuality
P.O. Box 208
Mount Vernon, IA 52314

    Phone: 319-895-8407
    Fax: 319-895-6203

Sexuality Information and Education Council of the United States,
    Inc. (SIECUS)
University of Pennylvania
Graduate School of Education
3700 Walnut Street
Philadelphia, PA 19104-6216

    Web access: http://www.siecus.org

Community Resources, continued:

The American Psychological Association or Your State Psychological Association (Telephone Book Blue Pages)

Your State Professional Licensure Board (psychiatrists, psychologists, social workers, clinical nurse specialists, professional counselors, marriage and family therapists)

The above national and state organizations can refer you to qualified couples/sex therapists in your area, should you want consultation. Please be certain any therapist you consider has credentials *from your state licensure board.* Credentials from the American Association of Marriage and Family Therapists (AAMFT) and/or AASECT certified sex counselors and therapists will indicate expertise over and above a license to practice, and are required by some states.

Toning Your Orgasm Muscles

Toned orgasm muscles enhance orgasms. Dr. Arnold Kegel in 1940 prescribed exercises to strengthen the pubococcygeal (PC) muscles of men and women who leaked urine (usually when they laughed or coughed). These are the muscles with which you hold urine. Not only did patients report better urinary control, their orgasms became stronger. Middle-age and older men will find these exercises particularly useful. We now call these the "Kegel" or "PC muscle" exercises.

Men who exercise their PC muscles also report better control over their orgasms, even with premature or early ejaculation and retarded or delayed ejaculation. PC exercises can be practiced anywhere at almost any time (except while driving or operating equipment that requires your full attention).

To identify your PC muscles: Imagine sitting or standing at the toilet with your knees spread comfortably apart. Release and stop an imaginary flow of urine. PC muscles are the only muscles able to stop urine flow in this position. When you recognize them, you can practice in any position, unobserved: prone, sitting, standing, or walking.

The exercises can be done briefly, one to six times a day, divided into no more than five minutes at a time, and no more than fifteen minutes total in a day. Beginners should start with one minute or less and build gradually to five minutes over several weeks. Remember to stop or rest when muscles tire. This exercise is about pleasure, not endurance.

Like any other muscles, the PC gets painfully sore with too much exercise. Your goal is not to overexercise, but rather, to build muscle tone slowly, preferably over four to six weeks. If muscles get sore and soreness persists, cut the exercises back by at least 75% and check with your physician. If you practice with an erection, you will notice your penis bend in a particular direction.

This can be sensually pleasing to an anal receptive partner, and delightful during oral sex.

Exercise I: Contract and relax the PC muscles rapidly (not intensely). Begin with ten or fifteen brief, gentle contractions, build to twenty-five the first week, fifty the second, seventy-five the third, until you can do about 150 at the end of a month or two. Then, add Exercise II.

Exercise II: Contract the PC muscles, hold for four to eight seconds, then relax. Begin with five contractions and gradually build to about fifty. When you can do fifty with ease, add Exercise III.

Exercise III: Imagine a ping pong ball rests at the opening of your anus. Tighten your PC muscles as if to suck the ball slowly and deeply into the opening. Begin with about five strong "pulls" and build to about fifty. Less, if you get sore.

Exercising PC muscles is particularly important for men of any age who ejaculate too rapidly or too slowly, because you acquire a measure of ejaculatory control as you regain tone in your orgasm muscles. After you build tone with daily practice, you can develop a maintenance schedule of three times a week, depending on your age and health.

Evaluation

Male partner #1, age _____

Length of partnership _____

1. Please indicate your purpose(s) in using this workbook:

    ____ A. To help me explore personal questions or concerns.
    ____ B. To find deeper relatedness with my partner.
    ____ C. To satisfy my curiosity.
    ____ D. Because my teacher/friend/partner/therapist recommended it (circle all that apply).
    ____ E. To update my knowledge for relationship, work, school, career (circle all that apply).

2. Was the workbook personally beneficial?

    ____ A. Not at all, a waste of time and money.
    ____ B. Slightly, I got a little bit but not much.
    ____ C. Moderately, it was good in some respects.
    ____ D. Very much, I got a lot from doing it.
    ____ E. Greatly, I had a transformative experience.

3. Did you complete all of the exercises, including discussions?

    ☐ Yes   ☐ No

4. Did you talk about what it was like to discuss each topic, after each exercise?

    ☐ Yes   ☐ No

5. Which exercises were most valuable for you?

6. Which exercises were least valuable for you?

7. What changes would you recommend?

8. Are you interested in other sexuality workbooks for yourself, friends, or family?

_____ A. Singles
_____ B. Over 65
_____ C. Lesbian couples
_____ D. Heterosexual couples
_____ E. Physical disabilities or medical problems

Other comments?

Thank you for taking the time to complete this form.
Your response to this survey contributes to ongoing research.

Please return to:

Couples Enrichment Institute
P.O. Box 420114
Atlanta, GA 30342-0114

Evaluation

Male partner #2, age _____

Length of partnership _____

1. Please indicate your purpose(s) in using this workbook:

     ____ A. To help me explore personal questions or concerns.
     ____ B. To find deeper relatedness with my partner.
     ____ C. To satisfy my curiosity.
     ____ D. Because my teacher/friend/partner/therapist recommended it (circle all that apply).
     ____ E. To update my knowledge for relationship, work, school, career (circle all that apply).

2. Was the workbook personally beneficial?

     ____ A. Not at all, a waste of time and money.
     ____ B. Slightly, I got a little bit but not much.
     ____ C. Moderately, it was good in some respects.
     ____ D. Very much, I got a lot from doing it.
     ____ E. Greatly, I had a transformative experience.

3. Did you complete all of the exercises, including discussions?

     ☐ Yes   ☐ No

4. Did you talk about what it was like to discuss each topic, after each exercise?

     ☐ Yes   ☐ No

5. Which exercises were most valuable for you?

6. Which exercises were least valuable for you?

7. What changes would you recommend?

8. Are you interested in other sexuality workbooks for yourself, friends, or family?

_____ A. Singles
_____ B. Over 65
_____ C. Lesbian couples
_____ D. Heterosexual couples
_____ E. Physical disabilities or medical problems

Other comments?

Thank you for taking the time to complete this form.
Your response to this survey contributes to ongoing research.

Please return to:

Couples Enrichment Institute
P.O. Box 420114
Atlanta, GA 30342-0114

Don't Explode
Don't Cave In
Don't Leave

Quiet Yourself

Couples Enrichment Institute
P. O. Box 420114, Atlanta, GA 30342-0114

Notes

Notes

Notes

Notes

ORDER FORM

Fax orders: (404) 255-7439

Online orders: forcouples@mindspring.com

Postal orders: Couples Enrichment Institute
                 P.O. Box 420114
                 Atlanta, GA 30342-0114, USA

Visit our website at http://www.mindspring.com/~forcouples/index.html

Qty	*Journey Toward Intimacy*	Unit	Total
	A Handbook for Couples	$12.99	
	A Handbook for Lesbian Couples	$12.99	
	A Handbook for Gay Couples	$12.99	
	A Handbook for Singles	$12.99	
$2.00 shipping for first book and $.50 per book thereafter			
Total			

Payment enclosed:

☐ Check (amount in U.S. dollars): $_____

☐ _____ ____/____
    VISA or Mastercard Number   Expiration

Signature: _____

Print Name: _____

Shipping address: _____
               Street   Apt. No.

_____
City   State   Zip

I understand I may return any unused, resalable books for a complete refund.

ORDER FORM

Fax orders: (404) 255-7439

Online orders: forcouples@mindspring.com

Postal orders: Couples Enrichment Institute
                  P.O. Box 420114
                  Atlanta, GA 30342-0114, USA

Visit our website at http://www.mindspring.com/~forcouples/index.html

Qty	*Journey Toward Intimacy*	Unit	Total
	A Handbook for Couples	$12.99	
	A Handbook for Lesbian Couples	$12.99	
	A Handbook for Gay Couples	$12.99	
	A Handbook for Singles	$12.99	
$2.00 shipping for first book and $.50 per book thereafter			
Total			

Payment enclosed:

☐ Check (amount in U.S. dollars): $_____

☐ _____ ___/___
    VISA or Mastercard Number   Expiration

Signature: _____

Print Name: _____

Shipping address: _____
            Street   Apt. No.

_____
City   State   Zip

I understand I may return any unused, resalable books for a complete refund.